When HILLARY RODHAM CLINTON Played ICE HOCKEY

by RACHEL RUIZ   illustrated by STELIYANA DONEVA

PICTURE WINDOW BOOKS
a capstone imprint

When Hillary Rodham Clinton was 4 years old, she ran home crying.
A girl had bullied her. She didn't know what to do.
"Go back outside, and stand up to the girl," Hillary's mother said.

So Hillary did. And she returned home smiling.

"Suzy will be my friend!" she yelled happily.

Thanks to her parents, young Hillary quickly learned to stand up for herself. She learned to speak up for what was right. Those early lessons would come in handy later. They would help Hillary make life better for millions of people in need.

Hillary Diane Rodham was born on October 26, 1947, in Chicago, Illinois. She was the first of three children for Hugh and Dorothy Rodham.

Hillary always looked out for her little brothers, Hughie Jr. and Tony. Her mother told her she could do whatever boys did.

Hillary's father believed in hard work and a good education. "With those two things," he told his kids, "no dream is beyond reach."

When Hillary was 3 years old, the Rodhams moved outside Chicago to Park Ridge. The neighborhood was fun. Nearly 50 kids lived on the block.

In winter, a neighbor made an ice rink in his backyard. All the kids gathered to skate and play hockey.

During summer, Hillary and the other kids played softball and kickball in the street. They used the sewer covers as bases.

Summer also meant trips to Pennsylvania for Hillary and her family. They stayed at a cabin on Lake Winola.

Hillary's father and grandpa had built the cabin themselves. It had no heat, bathtub, or shower. Hillary's father took his family there for a reason: He wanted them to know a life that was not as fancy as the one they had in Park Ridge.

Hillary loved her father. But he could be tough on his kids. One day Hillary brought home all A's and one B on her report card. She expected her father to be proud. Instead he said, "Maybe your school is too easy."

Hillary was saddened by her father's words. But she later said those words made her work harder in school.

Hillary's mother expected her children to do well in school too. She also pushed them to learn about the world by reading books. A trip to the library every week was a treat for Hillary.

Hillary had no trouble reading. But she did have trouble seeing things that were far away. She started wearing glasses when she was 9 years old.

As she got older, some people said mean things about how she looked. They said she should get contact lenses. She should dress in trendy clothes. She should wear makeup. Others did not like her hair.

Sometimes the comments hurt. But Hillary did not let other people stop her from being herself. She remembered her mother's words: "You are unique."

Hillary practiced her leadership skills at an early age. She earned many merit badges as a Girl Scout. She led bake sales and food drives. She put on neighborhood sporting events. She set up backyard carnivals. The money raised went to charities.

Hillary discovered that she liked to lead.

In the early 1960s, President John F. Kennedy wanted to send an American to the moon. Fourteen-year-old Hillary wrote a letter to the space agency, NASA. She wanted to lead the way by becoming an astronaut.

NASA wrote back. They said women were not allowed in the space program. Hillary felt sad. It was the first time that she could not meet a goal with her strong will and hard work.

The following year, Hillary and other kids from the local Methodist church went to hear Dr. Martin Luther King Jr. speak. Dr. King was a civil rights leader. He fought for the rights of black people throughout the United States.

Hillary listened to Dr. King talk about segregation. She thought about the teachings of her church. Methodists believed segregation and racism were wrong. Hillary decided that someday she would try to bring people together.

Hillary's wish to lead and to help people moved her to run for vice president of her 11th-grade class.
She won.

The following year, she ran for class president. She was the only girl in the election. The campaign was tough. Hillary said some of the boys didn't play fair, and she lost. One of the boys said she was **"really stupid if [she] thought a girl could be elected president."**

After hearing those words, Hillary was even more driven to win her next election.

Hillary went to college at Wellesley, an all-women's school in Massachusetts. Once again she ran for president of the student body. This time, she won. At her graduation ceremony in 1969, she gave a speech.

Hillary spoke powerfully about the country's problems. She said, **"Fear is always with us, but we just don't have time for it. Not now."**

Her classmates clapped for seven minutes. *Life Magazine*, one of the most popular magazines at the time, printed parts of her speech.

After college, Hillary went to Yale Law School. She wanted to be a lawyer. She wanted to protect the rights of children. In the library one day, she met William (Bill) Jefferson Clinton. Bill was a law student too. They quickly found they had a lot in common.

Hillary and Bill married in 1975. They had a daughter in 1980 — Chelsea Victoria Clinton. Just as Hillary's mother had told her, Hillary told Chelsea she could be whatever she wanted to be.

In 1993, Bill Clinton became the 42nd president of the United States. Hillary became the first lady. But she did not give up being a lawyer. She was the first first lady to have a job outside the White House.

As first lady, Hillary worked to help Americans get better health care. She also helped women around the world.

In 2000, Hillary became a U.S. senator for the state of New York. Not long after, Hillary started dreaming bigger than ever. She was ready to run for president again — this time, of the United States!

AFTERWORD

In 2008, Hillary Rodham Clinton ran for president of the United States. She lost the Democratic nomination to Barack Obama. But after he won, President Obama asked Hillary to serve as secretary of state. She proudly accepted.

In 2016, Hillary made history again. She became the first woman in U.S. history to be a major party's candidate for president.

Hillary never forgot the values her parents taught her as a child. Those values have made her one of the greatest leaders our country has ever known.

GLOSSARY

astronaut—a space pilot or traveler

bully—to frighten or threaten someone

campaign—organized actions and events with a specific goal, such as being elected

charity—a group that raises money or collects goods to help people in need

civil rights—the rights that all people have to freedom and equal treatment under the law

Democratic—belonging to the Democratic Party, one of two major political parties in the United States

election—the process of choosing someone or deciding something by voting

lawyer—a person who is trained to advise people about the law

Methodist—a person who practices the religion of Methodism, a Christian faith

NASA—a U.S. government agency that runs the space program; abbreviation for National Aeronautics and Space Administration

nomination—the choice of a person to run for office

racism—the belief that one race is better than another race

secretary of state—the head of the U.S. State Department and the president's leading adviser in dealing with other countries

segregation—the practice of keeping groups of people apart, especially based on skin color

READ MORE

Alexander, Heather. *Who Is Hillary Clinton?* Who Was …? New York: Grosset & Dunlap, an imprint of Penguin Random House, 2016.

Markel, Michelle. *Hillary Rodham Clinton: Some Girls Are Born to Lead.* New York: Balzer + Bray, an imprint of HarperCollins Publishers, 2016.

CRITICAL THINKING
★ QUESTIONS ★

1. Name two childhood traits or abilities of Hillary Rodham Clinton. How do you think they helped her become a successful leader as an adult?

2. Did Hillary's parents try to help her become a strong, smart person, or did they try to stop her? Support your answer with three pieces of evidence from the text.

3. Name two times in Hillary's life when things didn't go her way. Explain her reactions to these events. What (if anything) did she do to improve or to reach her goal the next time?

INTERNET SITES

Use FactHound to find Internet sites related to this book.
Visit *www.facthound.com*
Just type in 9781515815730 and go.

Super-cool stuff!

Check out projects, games, and lots more at
www.capstonekids.com

OTHER TITLES IN
★ THIS SERIES ★

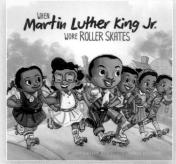  

INDEX

Special thanks to our adviser for his advice and expertise:
Timothy N. Thurber, Professor of History
Virginia Commonwealth University, Richmond, Virginia

Editor: Jill Kalz
Designer: Russell Griesmer
Creative Director: Nathan Gassman
Production Specialist: Katy LaVigne
The illustrations in this book were created digitally.

Editor's Note: Direct quotations in the main text are indicated by **bold** words.
Direct quotations are found on the following pages:
Page 3, line 2: Clinton, Hillary Rodham. *Living History.* New York: Scribner, 2004, p. 12.
Page 21, lines 3–4: Bernstein, Carl. *A Woman in Charge: The Life of Hillary Rodham Clinton.* New York: Vintage Books, 2008, p. 30.
Page 23, lines 4–5: Clinton, Hillary Rodham. *Living History.* New York: Scribner, 2004, p. 41.

Picture Window Books are published by Capstone, 1710 Roe Crest Drive, North Mankato, Minnesota 56003
www.mycapstone.com

Library of Congress Cataloging-in-Publication Data
Names: Ruiz, Rachel (Rachel Marie), author.
Title: When Hillary Rodham Clinton played ice hockey / by Rachel Ruiz ; illustrated by Steliyana Doneva.
Description: North Mankato, Minnesota : Picture Window Books, a Capstone imprint, 2018. |
Series: Leaders doing headstands | Audience: K to grade 3. | Includes bibliographical references and index.
Identifiers: LCCN 2017008203 | ISBN 9781515815730 (library binding) | ISBN 9781515815778 (paperback) | ISBN 9781515815815 (eBook PDF)
Subjects: LCSH: Clinton, Hillary Rodham—Childhood and youth—Juvenile literature. | Presidents' spouses—United States—Biography—
Juvenile literature. | Women presidential candidates—United States—Biography—Juvenile literature. | Stateswomen—United States—
Biography—Juvenile literature. | Women legislators—United States—Biography—Juvenile literature.
Classification: LCC E887.C55 R85 2018 | DDC 973.932092 [B]—dc23
LC record available at https://lccn.loc.gov/2017008203

Printed and bound in the United States of America.
010363F17

For Ashley x

Visit the author's website: www.ericjames.co.uk

Written by Eric James
Illustrated by Sara Sanchez
Designed by Nicola Moore

Published by Sourcebooks Jabberwocky, an imprint of Sourcebooks, Inc.
P.O. Box 4410, Naperville, Illinois 60567-4410
(630) 961-3900
Fax: (630) 961-2168
jabberwockykids.com

Date of Production: May 2017
Run Number: HTW_PO250717
Printed and bound in China (IMG)
10 9 8 7 6 5 4 3 2 1

Tiny the Rhode Island Easter Bunny

Written by
Eric James

Illustrated by
Sara Sanchez

sourcebooks
jabberwocky

One bright Easter morning,
while out for a jog,

Tiny hears,

"HELP!
I AM STUCK
IN A LOG."

He scratches his head,
thinking, "Who could that be?
It sounded like Fluff!
I had better go see."

Fluff's in a log
with her feet in the air.
"Hey, Fluff, what on earth
are you doing in there?"

A sad little voice
from an echoey space
says, "I thought this would make
a good egg-hiding place."

"You poor Easter Bunny,"
says Tiny, while giggling.
"I'll get you back out,
just hold tight and stop wriggling!"

Tiny pulls hard,
using all of his might.
He tries and he tries,
but his friend is stuck tight.

"My eggs," sighs poor Fluff.
"Who'll deliver them now?"
"I'll do it," says Tiny.
Fluff laughs and asks,

"How?!"

"Don't worry, dear Fluff.
Leave it all up to me.
I watched you last Easter.
How hard can it be?"

This bunny looks **funny...** Yes, something is **wrong!**

His feet are
too
big
and his
nose is too
long.

His skin
isn't
furry,
it's wrinkled
and rough.

His tail is
too thin,
and it's
NOT
made of fluff.

He's traveled through **Warwick**
and **Cranston** already.
He's all out of puff
and his legs feel unsteady.

He **hops**, then he stops,
then he **hops** a bit more,
then he stops all the **hopping...**

and **FLOPS**
to the floor!

"Hello," squeaks a mouse
in his fake bunny ear.
"Oh my, how you've grown
since I met you last year.
I'm Marvin, remember?
You're running quite late...
I'll help if you like."
Tiny nods and says,

"Great!"

They head down to **Newport** and rush through the streets, delivering handfuls of chocolatey treats.

Next **Portsmouth**, **Providence**,
and **Middletown** too.
There's not much time left
but there's SO MUCH to do!

"Speed up," Marvin squeaks,
"or we'll finish too late!
DIG under that hedge and
HOP over that gate."

This **Barrington** house has a fence all around. Poor Tiny tries digging down into the ground.

But the hole is too small (or his body's too big).
"How odd," Marvin thinks. "I thought bunnies could **dig!**"

This **Westerly** house
has a really high wall.
"Jump up," Marvin squeaks.
"C'mon, give it your all!"

So Tiny
jumps up but comes
down with a **THUMP!**
"How odd," Marvin thinks.
"I thought bunnies
could **JUMP!**"

"There's something not right,"
Marvin says. "Let me see..."
He scratches his chin and thinks,
"What can it be?"

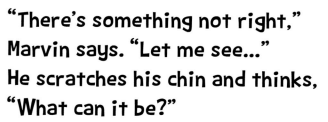

"You're not very fast—
well, just look at those legs!
You're not very careful.
You've cracked half the eggs!"

"You do not have whiskers!
You're no good at hopping!
Those ears look quite fake,
and that's **no** bunny dropping!"

"Aha! Now I've got it!"
He jumps to his toes.
"No bunny is born with a
trunk for a nose!"

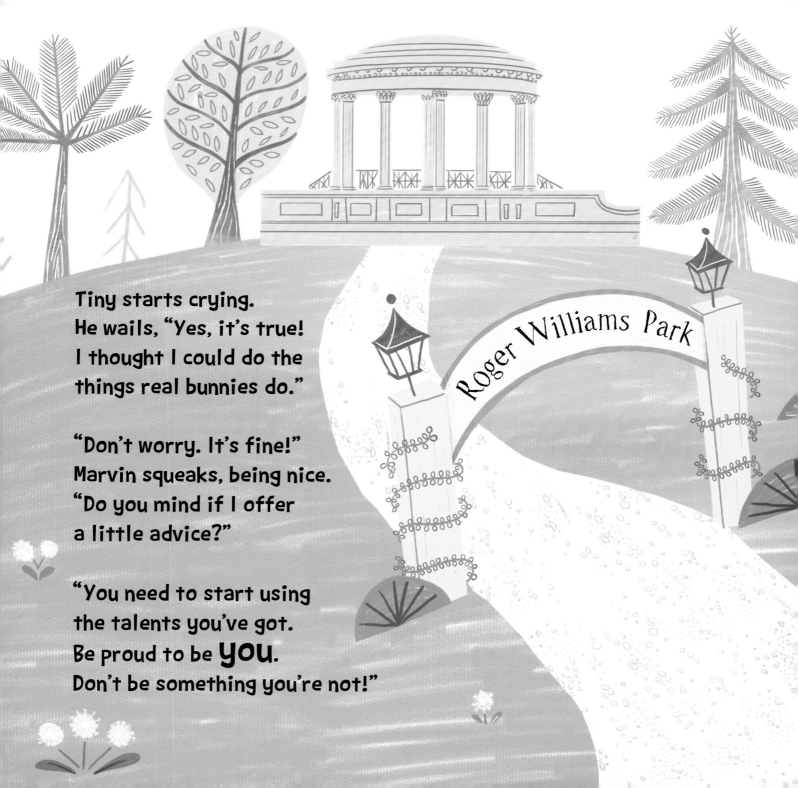

Tiny starts crying.
He wails, "Yes, it's true!
I thought I could do the
things real bunnies do."

"Don't worry. It's fine!"
Marvin squeaks, being nice.
"Do you mind if I offer
a little advice?"

"You need to start using
the talents you've got.
Be proud to be **you**.
Don't be something you're not!"

Roger Williams Park

"What talents?" says Tiny.
"What things can I do?"
He blows his big nose
and then aah...

aaah...

ACHOOOOOO!

"Eureka!" squeaks Marvin
from high in a tree.
"That wonderful,
big trunky nose
is the key!"

"It's strong and it's long.
It can pick things up, too.
It's perfect for seeing
this Easter job through."

"We'll put it to work
just as soon as we can.
Let's head to **Woonsocket**
and test out this plan."

This house has a fence,

and this house has a wall,

but with Tiny's big nose, there's no problem at all!

His long nose lifts up,
reaches over the top,
and he drops an egg down
on the lawn with a

P
l
o
P!

And look at the hole
in this fence...that'll do!
There's room for an egg
and a trunk to fit through.

Now the job seems quite easy. (Well, that's how it goes
when an elephant uses his brains and his nose.)

But daylight is breaking.
The sun starts to rise,
and home after home
stands in front of their eyes.

"I don't think we'll make it,"
squeaks Marvin. "Oh, dear!"
"Hang on," Tiny shouts.
"I've a marvelous idea!"

He sucks all the Easter eggs
into his nose,
and when his trunk's full
he takes aim...then he BLOWS!

Look at those eggs blasting out of his trunk, landing on lawns with a

THUNK!

THUNK!

THUNK!

THUNK!

The basket's soon empty.
"We did it, hooray!
Come on, let's help Fluff.
Oh, I hope she's okay."

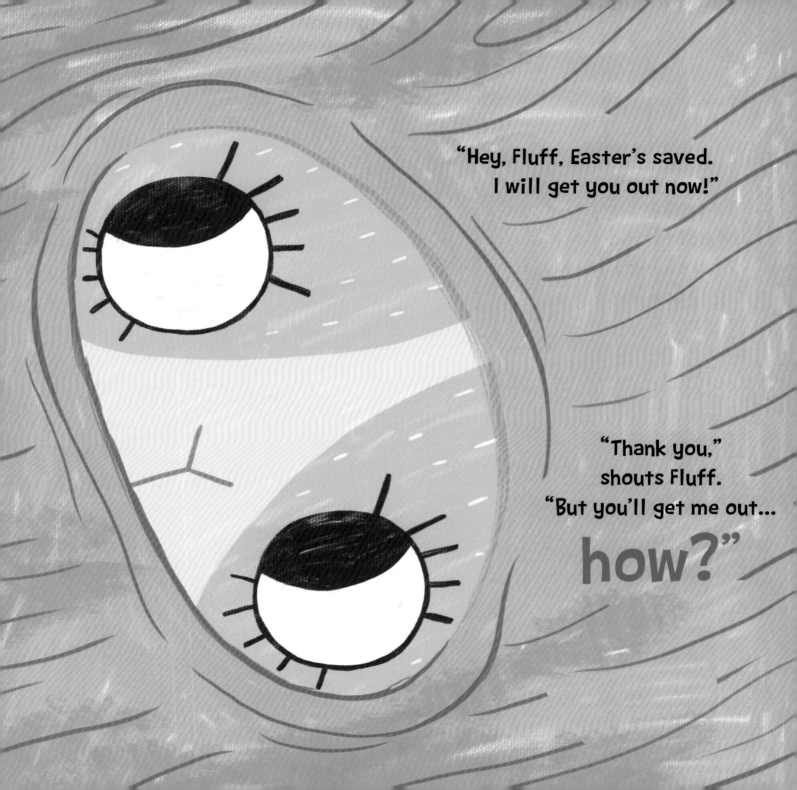

At the side
of the pond,
Tiny dips in
his trunk.
He drinks and
he drinks
till the water's
all drunk!

And using
his nose
as a huge
water hose,
he blows
through the log...

Look at Fluff!

UP she goes!

Happy Easter, Rhode Island

How many Easter eggs
are in this picture?